MYANMAR

A PORTRAIT OF

MYANMAR

Photography by Mark Downey
Text by Joe Cummings

AVA HOUSE

Published and distributed in
Myanmar by
AVA Publishing House.
2220/8 Ramkhamhaeng 36/1 Road,
Huamark, Bangkok 10240, Thailand.
Tel. (662) 375-2685-6, 732-0243-5
Fax (662) 375-2669
email: ava @ bps. book. co.th

Text and captions by Joe Cummings

Photography by **Mark Downey** except for photos by **Daniel Kahrs** appearing on pages 10, 11, 12-13, 26(bottom), 28-29, 30(bottom), 34(top and bottom), 35, 37(top and bottom), 40, 41, 49(top), 50(top), 51(bottom), 56(top), 57, 63(top and bottom), 64-65, 67(bottom), 73(top), and 76(top). Photos by **Joe Cummings** appear on pages 20(bottom), 24, 36, 48(top), 49(bottom), 53(bottom), 59(bottom), 62, 66(bottom), 67(top), 68(bottom), 73(bottom), 75(top and bottom), and 76(bottom). Additional photography by **Christopher C. Burt** on pages 5 and 14; **Luca Tettoni** on page 72, and **John Elk** on page 25.

Architectural renderings by Dept. of Architecture, Rangoon Institute of Technology.

Designed and produced by Christopher C. Burt, Pacific Rim Press
Cartography by Mark Stroud

Production House : Twin Age Limited
4/F., 20 Hollywood Rd., Central, Hong Kong
Printed in China

ISBN 962-7987-06-8

Dedication:
I would like to pay tribute to the warmth, generosity and spirit of the Burmese People—without which the photographs in this book would not be possible.
—Mark Downey

Half-title page
The sun sets over Mandalay Fort, final stronghold of the Burmese monarchy prior to the 19th-century British takeover.

Title page
The Mon, an ethnic group native to Lower Burma, built Shwemawdaw Paya, one of the largest and most sacred of all Burmese pagodas, over a thousand years ago. Said to contain a sacred tooth relic of the Buddha, the central stupa towers 91 metres over the city of Bago—making it higher than even Shwedagon Paya in Yangon.

Right
One of the hallmarks of Burmese art includes a tendency to add crowns, ornate chestpieces, and other royal attire to sculptural renditions of the Buddha. The upraised hand signifies the abhaya mudra, a standard gesture understood to mean 'Have no fear.'

Following pages
A Buddhist monk walks calmly through a crowded market in Mandalay after his morning alms-round. Theravada Buddhism—followed by over 80% of the nation—forbids monks from tilling the soil or preparing their own food. Instead each monk relies entirely on the generosity of the Buddhist laity to place a few handfuls of rice and curry into his black-lacquered almsbowls for the monk's entire daily sustenance.

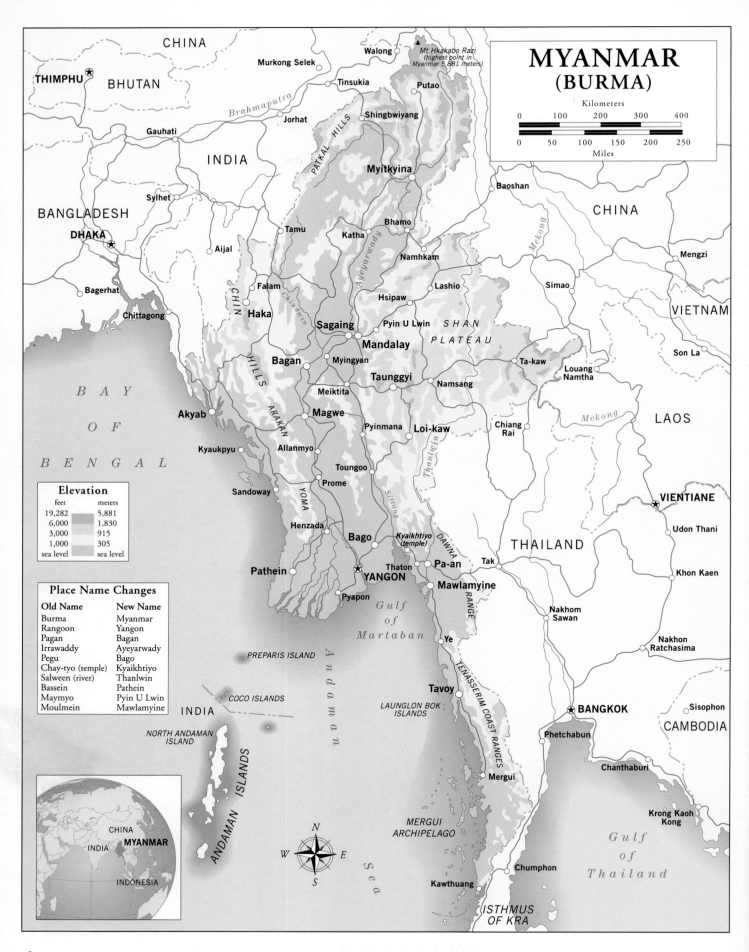

MYANMAR
(BURMA)

Kilometers
0 100 200 300 400

Miles
0 50 100 150 200 250

CHINA

THIMPHU
BHUTAN

Murkong Selek

Walong

Mt Hkakabo Razi
(highest point in
Myanmar 5,881 meters)

Tinsukia

Putao

Baoshan

CHINA

Brahmaputra

Jorhat

Shingbwiyang

PATKAL HILLS

Myitkyina

Mengzi

Gauhati

INDIA

Bhamo

Namhkam

Simao

VIETNAM

BANGLADESH

Sylhet

Tamu

Katha

Aijal

DHAKA

Bagerhat

Falam

Chittagong

CHIN

Haka

HILLS

Ayeyarwady

Chindwin

Lashio

Hsipaw

Pyin U Lwin

SHAN

PLATEAU

Ta-kaw

Son La

Sagaing

Mandalay

Namsang

Louang
Namtha

Bagan

Myingyan

Taunggyi

Meiktita

Namsang

BAY

OF

BENGAL

Akyab

Kyaukpyu

ARAKAN

Magwe

Pyinmana

Loi-kaw

Chiang
Rai

Mekong

LAOS

Allanmyo

YOMA

Sandoway

Toungoo

Prome

Thanlwin

VIENTIANE

Udon Thani

Elevation

feet	meters
19,282	5,881
6,000	1,830
3,000	915
1,000	305
sea level	sea level

Henzada

Bago

Kyaikhtiyo
(temple)

Sittang

DAWNA

Pa-an

Tak

THAILAND

Khon Kaen

Place Name Changes

Old Name	New Name
Burma	Myanmar
Rangoon	Yangon
Pagan	Bagan
Irrawaddy	Ayeyarwady
Pegu	Bago
Chay-tyo (temple)	Kyaikhtiyo
Salween (river)	Thanlwin
Bassein	Pathein
Maymyo	Pyin U Lwin
Moulmein	Mawlamyine

Pathein

Pyapon

Thaton

YANGON

Mawlamyine

Ye

Gulf
of
Martaban

RANGE

Nakhom
Sawan

Nakhon
Ratchasima

PREPARIS ISLAND

TENASSERIM COAST RANGES

Andaman

COCO ISLANDS

Tavoy

LAUNGLON BOK
ISLANDS

Bangkok

Sisophon

INDIA

NORTH ANDAMAN
ISLAND

ANDAMAN ISLANDS

Phetchabun

CAMBODIA

Chanthaburi

Mergui

MERGUI
ARCHIPELAGO

Krong Kaoh
Kong

Sea

Gulf
of
Thailand

CHINA

INDIA

MYANMAR

INDONESIA

N
W   E
S

Chumphon

Kawthuang

ISTHMUS
OF KRA

INTRODUCTION

This is Burma, and it will be quite unlike any land you know about.

-Rudyard Kipling, *Letters from the East,* 1898

For centuries Myanmar has exemplified all that's exotic about the East—amazing Marco Polo in the 13th century, the Portuguese 300 years later, and the British after yet another three centuries. Virtually shut off from the outside world by political and economic instability since 1948, much of the country has only recently been opened to foreign visitors.

The country's self-imposed isolation has led fanciful travel writers to dub Myanmar the 'Forgotten Land' but to the Burmese it has always been the 'Golden Land' or *Shwe Pyi Daw.* Shimmering bell-shaped pagodas, gilded with layers of hand-pounded goldleaf, pierce the skylines of every major city. In the countryside smaller pagodas covered in silver, copper, or whitewash cling to the slopes, peaks, and riverbanks wherever the Buddhist faithful are found.

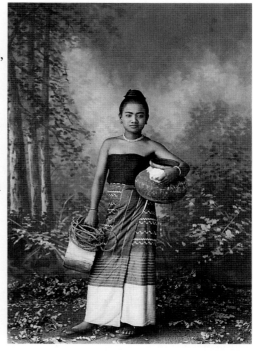

The largest country in mainland Southeast Asia, Myanmar spreads across 676,000 square kilometers of mountains, plateaus, plains, river valleys, and sea coasts. From east to west, Myanmar measures around 1,000 kilometers at its widest point, while from north to south it extends roughly twice that distance. Reaching into the country's northern end, the southernmost tip of the Himalayan Range posts mountain peaks such as 5,889-meter Hkakabo Razi—the highest mountain in Southeast Asia—and several other snowcapped pinnacles over 5,000 meters. The Tropic of Cancer bisects this region just above Myitkyina in the Kachin State; the rest of the country, all the way south to the Malay Peninsula's Isthmus of Kra on the Thailand-Myanmar border, falls within the tropics.

Myanmar's 2,830-kilometer coastline undulates northwest to southeast along the Bay of Bengal, Gulf of Martaban, and Andaman Sea—all part of the huge Indian Ocean marine complex. Thousands of continental, delta, and oceanic islands dot the seas, including a group of over 800 idyllic and as yet undeveloped isles in the south known as the Mergui Archipelago.

Major rivers spring forth in the hilly northern highlands and flow southward into the sea creating vast and fertile floodplains where rice, fruit, and vegetables are cultivated in abundance. Myanmar's rivers not only provide food for its people, they are also the major thoroughfares for long-distance travel by riverboat. The 2,000-kilometer Ayeyarwady River (Irrawaddy) is navigable year round for at least three quarters of its length and its banks have served as sites for all of the country's major civilizations. During the colonial era, the British-owned Irrawaddy Flotilla Company transported as many as nine million passengers yearly on a huge fleet of wood-and-brass sternwheelers. Today the flotilla's legacy lives on in the hundreds of double-decker passenger boats plying the Ayeyarwady and other rivers, particularly in the vast delta area to the immediate west of Yangon.

The young woman posing in this hundred-year-old studio photo proudly displays the same type of longyi *or wraparound skirt worn by most women in Burma today. These colorful textiles are loom-woven of silk or cotton in thousands of different patterns which engender regional, ethnic, and class variation. Most costly and coveted are the* acheik *designs, which feature wavy or zigzag patterns and may incorporate a hundred or more spools of thread. Such* luntaya *('hundred spool')* acheik longyis *are so thick and sturdy they may stay in families for generations. Burmese women nowadays favor calf-length longyis, topped off by a waist-length, sleeved blouse.*

Burma's multi-ethnic population of 45 million includes around 65% Burmans, descendants of Tibeto-Burman immigrants who first settled Upper Myanmar in the 9th or 10th century AD. Nowadays this majority group for the most part occupies the plains and river valleys of the country's central states and divisions. The "frontier states"–those states bordering Thailand, Laos, China, India, and Bangladesh-are inhabited by the Shan (10%), Karen (7%), Rakhine (4%), and less numerous ethnic groups such as the Mon , Kayah, Kachin, and Chin. In the mountainous regions of northeastern Myanmar, where Laos, Myanmar, Thailand, and China meet, live a number of "hill tribes" –Lahu, Lisu, Palaung, Danu, Pa-O, Kaw, and others. Cities with a strong British colonial heritage also boast significant numbers of Indian and Chinese descendants of civil servants imported by the Raj.

Although each ethnic group has its own language and share a common set of cultural characteristics known as *bamah-san chin* or "Burmese-ness" which serve as a code of behavior or social ideal for most Burmese citizens regardless of their ethnic background. These include respect for elders, familiarity with the Buddhist tripitaka or Pali scriptures, fluency in the Burmese language, modest dress, discreet behavior toward the opposite sex, and the cultivation of a quiet, subtle, and indirect nature.

Myanmar's historical roots extend to the early kingdom of Suvannabhumi ("Golden Land"), a loose collection of agricultural states established by the Mon among the fertile river deltas of Lower Myanmar, Thailand, and Cambodia around 2500 years ago. Sometime during the early first millennium a group called the Pyus migrated southward from the Tibetan plateau and developed the elaborate walled cities of Beikthano, Hanlin, and Thayekhittaya (Sri Ksetra) in Upper Myanmar. Like the Mon, the Pyu were Buddhists, and they built sturdy brick-and-stucco shrines which later became the inspiration for the larger monuments of Bagan.

Former president Ne Win's policy of 'The Burmese Road to Socialism' between 1962 and 1989 did not preclude individual private enterprise. Markets such as this one near the northern city of Myitkyina have been flourishing continually for centuries.

In the 9th century, the Pyus were displaced by another Tibeto-Burman group from the north who established the kingdom of Bagan at a large bend in the Ayeyarwady River. Under King Anawrahta, who ascended the throne in 1044, Bagan incorporated architectural influences from the Pyu and religious principles from the Mon, gaining a vast number of tributary states in the process. The First Burmese Empire, as the Bagan era is known to the Burmese, lasted until the late 13th century when it declined rapidly due to dynastic weakening and the increasing power of adversaries to the north (Kublai Khan and his Mongols) and to the east (the Shans).

Following 250 years of dissolution, the Second Burmese Empire arose under King Bayinnaung and claimed even more territory than the First. Between 1551 and 1752 the capital shifted from Taungoo to Bago to Ava according to prevailing trade and defense conditions. A semi-independent kingdom called Mrauk U developed along the Bay of Bengal during this same era. Prosperity brought on by trade alliances with India, Holland, Spain, and Portugal allowed Mrauk U kings to build numerous religious monuments which today are rivaled only by those of ancient Bagan.

Mon usurpers captured Ava in 1752 but after eight years of warfare the Third Burmese Empire ushered in the last of Myanmar's monarchical ruling clans, who built their capitals in and around Mandalay. In 1767 King Hsinbyushin, invaded Siam and brought back hundreds of Thai artisans,

A worker carries a midday meal to her family working on a construction site.

dancers, and musicians to create the greatest cultural infusion the country had seen since the 11th-century defeat of Thaton. In an increasingly expansionist mode, the next Burmese king took Mrauk U and the Rakhine territory along the Indian border, an act which raised the ire of the neighboring British Raj.

The British reacted by annexing the Rakhine and Taninthayi territories in the Anglo-Burmese War of 1824; subsequent wars in 1852 and 1886 completed the British takeover of the entire country as Burma became part of the Raj. The Burmese royal family were exiled to India and Burma remained a British colony until the Japanese invaded during World War II.

Burmese nationalism grew during the war, and once the Japanese forces had been expelled the Burmese demanded independence from Britain. Independence was gained in 1948 but proved problematic when the northern frontier states didn't receive the autonomy promised them by the British and by Myanmar's own Panglong Agreement of 1947. Ethnic insurgencies formed in the Chin, Kachin, Shan, Kayin and Kayah and still exist today, though all but the Shan have agreed to forsake armed struggle against the Yangon government.

Nearly 90% of all Burmese practice Theravada Buddhism, the world's oldest and most traditional Buddhist sect. Burmese Buddhists believe that individuals work out their own paths to *nibbana* through a combination of good works, meditation, and study of the *dhamma* or Buddhist philosophy. Although monasticism plays a major role in the religion, priests aren't considered necessary intermediaries between the faithful and full realization of the Buddha's Middle Way.

Burmese Buddhist men are expected to shave their heads and temporarily don the red robes of the Sangha or monkhood at least once in their lives. Many enter the Sangha twice, first as a novice in their pre-teen years and again as a fully ordained monk sometime after the age of 20. Pre-teen girls may undergo a similar

A monastery south of Mandalay specializes in the manufacture of Buddha images.

temporary novitiation as Buddhist nuns or, more commonly, they will participate in a simple initiation ceremony involving the piercing of their ears. For boys and girls, such ceremonies–known as *shin pyu* to the Burmese–are major social events that may entail horse- or elephant-back processions, music and dance performances, and the "possession" of spirit mediums in trance.

Spirit worship in Myanmar predates Buddhism and is still practiced throughout most of the country, even by Buddhists. The Burmese believe that *nats* or animistic spirits inhabit lakes, streams, trees, mountains and other natural features, and that these nats must be placated whenever humans trespass upon or makes use of said features. Small nat shrines may be built at the edge of rice fields, behind houses, or beneath trees specifically to receive offerings-rice, coconuts, bananas, flowers, cups of water-from nearby residents or passers-by.

In addition to nature spirits, there is a separate class of 37 nats thought to have descended from historical personages, including kings, queens, yogis, and other noble humans who died in tragic circumstances, typically suicide, murder, or macabre accidents. Shrines to these nats feature mannequin-like figures in bright costume representing the individual nats; they are commonly seen as adjunct shrines in larger pagoda compounds. The principal abode of the 37 nats, a rock outcropping called Mt. Popa, lies east of Bagan and is the site of several spirit festivals throughout the year. Every nat-worshipper in Myanmar hopes to make a pilgrimage to Mt. Popa at least once in their lives. Most Burmese see no conflict between nat worship and Buddhism believing that the former is as necessary for this life as the latter is for the next life.

In addition to Mt. Popa, every Burmese and every visitor to Myanmar wants to experience the archaeological grandeur of Bagan, where over 2,000 temple ruins spread across 40 kilometers of flat plain along a sharp bend of the upper Ayeyarwady River. Erected over a 300-year period between the 9th and 13th centuries, the brick-and-stucco monuments range from small and delicately ornamented structures like Ananda Ok Kyaung or Pitaka Taik to the soaring, cathedral-like Ananda or Sulamani temples, considered among the greatest works of architecture in Asia.

A day's ferry ride upriver is Mandalay, Myanmar's cultural heart and the second largest city in the country. At rambling Zegyo, the city's "Central Market", vendors purvey handicrafts-textiles, silverwork, jewelry, basketry, pottery, clothing, and *kalaga* (a Burmese tapestry) from all over Myanmar, as well as imported merchandise from India, China, and Thailand. The restored Mandalay Palace, at the city's north end, offers visitors an architectural perspective of Myanmar's last royal dynasty. At the other end of the city, the shrine complex of Mahamuni Paya contains one of the most highly revered Buddha images in Myanmar, a huge half-millennium-old sitting figure covered with a 15-centimeter-thick layer of goldleaf accumulated over centuries of worship.

(Previous pages) *Dusk settles over the sleepy river port of Sagaing. The Ayeyarwady remains one of the principle transport links between Mandalay and Yangon providing the only link to the outside world for many small comunities.*

Other former royal capitals near Mandalay–Ava, Amarapura, and Sagaing–offer historic ruins of palaces, monasteries, and pagodas in more pastoral settings. At Mingun, an hour's sampan journey north, stand the ruins of one of the world's largest Buddhist pagodas, a 50-metre brick goliath begun at the end of the 18th century and half-destroyed by earthquake in 1838. The hour-long trip to Mingun provides visitors with a fine sampling of Burmese river life.

Remnants of the Raj grace the town of Pyin U Lwin–known as Maymyo during the colonial era, when perspiring British officers used this cool "hill station" as a holiday retreat-in the highlands northeast of Mandalay. Brightly painted, horse-drawn coaches, the main form of local transport, clip-clop along streets lined with Tudor mansions, red-brick churches, and other colonial architecture. Trees and flowering plants native to temperate climates thrive alongside tropical flora at the town's Botanical Garden, the only one of its kind in Myanmar.

Further east on the Shan Plateau, surrounded by mountains and high river valleys, vast Inle Lake offers a complete change of scenery. The Intha, an ethnic group unique to the lake area, fish Inle's shallow waters from graceful teak canoes, which they often paddle while standing up; they use their legs as well as their arms to ward off fatigue while paddling the lake's lengthy distances. The Intha's diet of freshwater fish is supplemented by vegetables cultivated on the lake's artificial "floating" islands, made by clumping soil together with water hyacinth and staking the resulting masses to the lake floor with bamboo poles. The Intha are also known for skillful silk-weaving and for the crafting of colorful cloth shoulder bags.

A journey through the Ayeyarwady River delta and along the Bay of Bengal coast will reward the visitor with perspectives of Myanmar's largest pottery works in Twante near Yangon, the historic inland port of Pathein, and the quiet beachside villages of Letkhokkon, Chaungtha, Gwa, and Ngapali. Beyond Ngapali near the Bangladesh border, in the Rakhine State, the 13th- to 15th-century temple ruins at Mrauk U rival those at Bagan in their awesome size and majesty.

In Yangon, the nation's capital, Shwedagon Paya, a Mon-built stupa dating to the founding of the city in the mid-18th century, is the single most important religious monument in Myanmar. It floats above the city's green skyline like an inverted golden ice-cream cone. Tree-lined boulevards radiating in all directions from Shwedagon lead to other gilded stupas and hallowed monasteries, as well as landscaped lakes, public gardens, the broad Yangon River, and bustling market venues such as the immense Bogyoke Aung San Market.

The road north of Yangon splits at Taukkyan; one fork continues north to Mandalay while another bends east around the Gulf of Martaban to Bago, a town of historic Mon and Burman pagodas as well as one of the largest reclining Buddha figures in the world. Further east atop Mt. Kyaikhtiyo a seven-meter gilded boulder balances on the edge of a granite cliff 1,200 meters above the coastal plains. Said to be magically held in place by a Buddha hair enshrined in a small stupa mounting the rock, Kyaikhtiyo is the second holiest Buddhist site in Myanmar after Shwedagon Paya. A strenuous four-hour walk along the 11-kilometer path up the mountain confers great merit upon pilgrims; the infirm or less devoted may ride in public trucks to within a 45-minute walk of the summit, then complete the journey atop bamboo palanquins borne on the shoulders of well-paid carriers. Sunrise or sunset, the view from the shrine is one of the most beautiful in Myanmar if not all Southeast Asia.

Mawlamyine (known to most of the English-speaking world as Moulmein) sits at the northeastern end of the Gulf of Martaban at the mouth of the Thanlwin River. This sleepy tropic port boasts a number of well-endowed Mon Buddhist temples, a cultural museum, pagoda-studded islands, and fading colonial architecture. Among the Burmese the city is known for markets filled with fresh betelnut, durian, coconuts, and mangoes. Myanmar's uniqueness becomes more strongly apparent the longer one travels in the country. Whether visitors take the time to experience a little or a lot, one always departs with the feeling that there is much more to explore.

Rangoon. River Scene.

During the 1826-1947 British annexation of Burma to the Raj, the colonial administration constructed numerous railways, tram lines, and motorways to facilitate commerce and transport within the country. The British also introduced the Irrawaddy Flotilla, a huge fleet of double-decked paddle steamers that plied 8000 kilometers of navigable Burmese rivers. Today the IF's heir, the Inland Water Transport Company, continues to operate over 500 double-deckers converted to diesel power.

(Previous pages) *A man prepares to prostrate himself three times before Yangon's Shwedagon Paya, once each for the Buddha, the Dhamma, and the Sangha—the teacher, the teachings, and the Buddhist community. Visits to Buddhist temples in Burma are most commonly planned to coincide with the fortnightly full and new moons, considered holy days on the Buddhist lunar calendar. More devout Buddhists may attend on a daily basis to practice meditation or to make offerings of candles, incense, and flowers.*

Hpoongyees in tram car returning with alms collected

The British legacy included such colonial relics as the exclusive Pegu Club pictured below where the colonialists could relax in in tropical style while enjoying all the comforts of home.

Pegu Club — Rangoon.

The British colonial legacy lives on in Burma's larger cities, whose main avenues are lined with Raj-era architecture. The Strand (below), near the Yangon River waterfront in downtown Yangon, remains one of the oldest and most prestigious hotel addresses in Southeast Asia. Built in 1896 by the famous Sarkies brothers (who also designed Singapore's Raffles Hotel and Bangkok's Oriental Hotel), The Strand was one of the glories of the British Raj prior to World War II, when it was temporarily forced to close. Following Burma's 1948 independence, the hotel changed back and forth between private and government ownership until 1991, when Dutch-Indonesian entrepreneur Adrian Zecha gave The Strand a massive facelift.

(Right) Barefoot worshipers cluster around a 'planetary post' at Shwedagon Paya. Most larger stupas—the central spired monument or 'pagoda'—are surrounded by eight planetary posts, one for each day of the Burmese week. Thursday through Tuesday coincide with the Western calendar, while Wednesday is divided into two days—Wednesday morning (when the Buddha is thought to have been born) and Wednesday afternoon. Each day is associated with a particular planet and animal; Wednesday morning, for example, coincides with the planet Mercury and the tusked elephant.

Yangon, formerly known as Rangoon, has intrigued visitors ever since Burma went into its self-imposed isolation during the 1960s and 70s. In recent years the city has undergone a major facelift since the opening of its doors to foriegn investment. The Supreme Court Building (right) is a glorious example of colonial architecture which has been well preserved inspite of the vicissitudes of time.

(Previous pages) At every religious monument in Burma, lay volunteers handle all maintenance, including the daily cleaning of the compound and necessary repairs. Here the central stupa at Shwedagon Paya undergoes its annual regilding. Since its 1769 construction, the stupa has accumulated an estimated 53 metric tons of goldleaf. By religious custom, the wearing of shoes is forbidden inside all temple, pagoda, or monastery compounds.

(Above and right) *From dawn to dusk, urban life in Burma centers around its markets and street vendors. Abundant fresh fruits–tropical varieties such as bananas, pomelos, and durian from the south, temperate fruits like strawberries and grapes from the north–find their way to virtually every corner of the country.*

(Left) *Home-grown cottage industries supply textiles, pottery, metalware—even these children's masks laid out by a young vendor in Mandalay—used in everyday life.*

(Following pages) *On a dry flat plain along a sharp bend in the Ayeyarwady River, Bagan boasts over 2,000 ancient religious sites in a 40-square-kilometer area. Founded in AD 1057 by King Anawrahta as Burma's first truly Burman kingdom, the Buddhist city-state thrived little longer than 200 years but has left behind an architectural splendor that ranks among the most impressive of artistic endeavors in human history.*

The artistry and craftsmanship displayed at Bagan is unequaled in pre-colonial Southeast Asia. Most monuments consist of carefully assembled, mortarless brick cores covered with delicately engraved stucco. Some temples feature masterfully carved sandstone reliefs illustrating a variety of Buddhist and Hindu subjects—the latter are always depicted as paying homage to the former. The square-cornered, corncob-shaped sikhara or superstructure atop Abeyadana Temple (above) is typical of early Bagan (c. AD 850-1120) monuments.

Several thriving villages—Myinkaba, Thiripyitsaya, Wetkyi-In, Tetthe—surround the archaeological zone, where horse- or oxen-drawn carts serve as the main form of transportation. Shwezigon Paya (right), seen in the background, is Bagan's oldest and most well-maintained religious monument.

(Above) *The 19th-century Shinpin-Sharjho Monastery near Salay, to the south of Bagan on the same side of the river, is one of the oldest surviving wooden monasteries in Burma. In a country where most meals are cooked over open fires, structures made of wood frequently succumb to stray sparks. Young novice monks are walking beneath the main hall, which is held aloft by 170 teak pillars.*

(Left) *Flower-festooned, burgundy-dyed parasols shade the heads of young men on their way to a monastic novitiation ceremony. Most traditional Burmese parasols and umbrellas hail from the delta port of Pathein, where around 25 workshops hand-craft nearly the entire national supply.*

(Right) *A monk studies Buddhist scripture in front of the exquisitely carved 140 year old doors of Shwe Imbin Monastery in the ancient capital city of Ava.*

(Left) *A huge reclining Buddha nearly fills the surrounding shrine hall at Manuha Paya in the village of Myinkaba, Bagan Archaeological Zone. One of the oldest temples in Bagan, Manuha is named for a Mon king who was taken prisoner of war by King Anawrahta's Burman army in the 11th century. The image's long, aquiline nose exemplifies classic Bagan Buddhist sculpture.*

(Above) *Carved wooden cabinets such as these—gilded and painted in the traditional Burmese style—contain collections of Buddhist scriptures called* tripitaka. *The Pali term means 'three baskets' and refers to the three components of the Theravada Buddhist canon: the Sutta (sayings of the Buddha), Vinaya (monastic discipline), and Abhidhamma (Buddhist psychology / philosophy). All Burmese Buddhists can recite at least a few verses of the tripitaka from memory.*

(Right) *A well-worn teak carving at Yoe Soe Monastery in Salay depicts an episode from one of the birth stories or jataka of the Buddha. Jataka scenes serve as the single most popular theme for temple decoration, whether in mural painting, bas relief, or sculpture. Today Burmese wood-carvers also produce more secular themes for the growing tourist market.*

40

(Previous pages) *Mt. Popa, a granite outcropping atop an extinct volcano, thrusts above the plains between Bagan and Mandalay. Among the Burmese, the entire mountain and its surrounding forests are known as the domain of Burma's most powerful nats or spirit-world entities. These spirits are heir to a pre-Buddhist era in Burma when the main form of religious expression consisted of placating animistic spirits associated with hills, trees, rivers, caves, and other features of the natural landscape. King Anawrahta's efforts to ban nat worship and force 'pure' Theravada Buddhism upon the Burmese during the 11th century failed, and today most Burmese practice a seamless amalgam of animism and Buddhism. Shrines along the base of Mt. Popa contain mannequin-like images of the 37 principal nats, while the loftier shrines at the summit itself are reserved for Buddhist worship.*

(Above and right) *Of the vast nat pantheon present in everyday Burmese life, the foremost 37 are believed by the Burmese to be descended from noble humans, including several historic personages in the Thai and Burmese monarchies who died over a thousand years ago. Coconuts and bananas make the most common offerings at nat shrines, but the Burmese believe individual nats have additional preferences--liquor and candles may be suitable for some nats, water and flowers for others. Two of the most famous of the Burmese nats, the 'Muslim Brothers' Byat-wi and Byat-ta, flank their mother Mae Wunna (above). Mae Wunna reigns as the patron nat of flowers and medicinal herbs, with Mt. Popa her principle fief; her sons also reside at Mt. Popa, but make annual journeys to Taungbyon near Mandalay, the site of the country's largest nat festival every August.*

(Above and right) *New Zegyo Market functions as the nerve center for Mandalay, business and cultural capital of Upper Burma. Because Mandalay stands at the crossroads of modern trade routes extending to India, China, and Thailand, the city's markets offer an immense variety of hand-crafted as well as manufactured merchandise. When this escalator was first unveiled in 1995, local residents stood in line to experience the thrill of motorized stair-climbing.*

(Left) *Longyis are always in demand for the men of Burma. The brightly colored lengths of cotton can be worn with any type of shirt, from T-shirts to Mandarin-collar dress shirts (or no shirt at all). They never go out of style, never need tailoring, and are easily loosened after a big meal.*

42

British officers and Indian troops parade outside the Mandalay Palace walls in 1890. When the British occupied Mandalay in 1885, the city had served as the royal capital for the country's last monarchy, headed by King Thibaw, since 1861. Mandalay Palace itself—surrounded by walls measuring three meters thick at the base and standing eight meters high—was assembled of dismantled wooden structures from previous royal palaces in nearby Amarapura. A shematic of the east elevation of the Palace buildings stretching some 650 feet (197 meters) is illsutrated below. The British renamed the facility Fort Dufferin and parceled the property into the Government House and the British Club, but the entire complex burned down during a fierce battle between British and Japanese troops in March 1945.

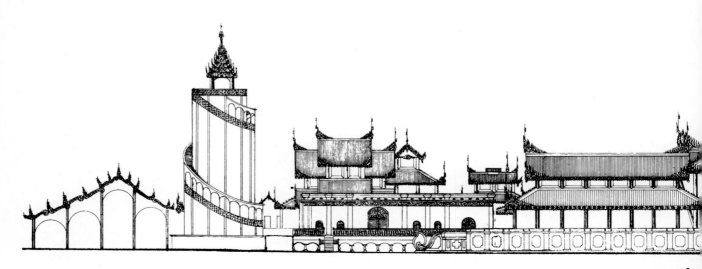

ပန္တလေးနန္းတေ
East Elevatio

Classical dancers perform before Prince Albert Victor during a visit to Mandalay in 1889. The girls are selected from wealthy local families and trained by a ballet master who can be seen seated on the left. The women behind him are ladies who once attended the Burmese royal family.

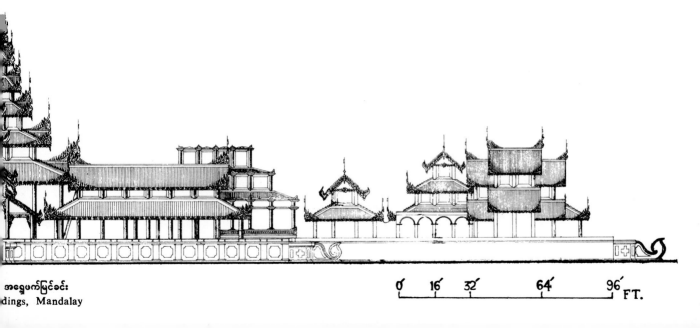

အရှေ့ဖက်မြင်ခင်း

dings, Mandalay

0′ 16′ 32′ 64′ 96′ FT.

(Above) *Just outside the walls of Mandalay Fort a 70-metre-wide moat extends for two kilometers along each side of the square fort plan. Today Burmese architects are rebuilding many of the palace buildings, using the original plans, to serve as a tourist attraction.*

(Left) *Decked out in sequined festival clothing, ear-rings, and a mock crown, a young man joins a* shin-pyu *or novitiation procession. Once the procession reaches the monastery, the boys will offer flowers to their monastic preceptors, who will initiate them into the Theravada Buddhist order as novice monks. The boy's princely attire symbolizes the royal life Siddhartha Gautama led before renouncing the world to become a wandering mendicant.*

(Right) *Rural residents depend on city markets as a sales outlet for the crops they cultivate in the fields and the handicrafts they fashion at home. Women who spend time outdoors often apply a paste of* thanaka—*a fragrant bark with skin-conditioning properties—to their faces. In addition to protecting one's face from the effects of the sun, the paste's swirling patterns are considered a mark of beauty. Loom-woven shoulder bags carry personal effects and come in many sizes, colors, and designs.*

(Above) *Older American and European vehicles, especially those from the pre-1962 era, are lovingly maintained by truck and bus drivers throughout Burma. When a Chevy body rusts beyond repair, discarded steel oil barrels may be hammered into a replacement.*

(Left) *A snack vendor hands a betelnut packet to a rail passenger on the Mandalay Express. Burma's meter-gauge railway extends 4,684 kilometers—as far north as Myitkyina in the Kachin State, and as far south as Yay on the Taninthayi Peninsula. Of the country's 318 locomotives, nearly 50 still run on steam. Rail travel is slow but in areas where there are no roads it's the only viable long-distance land transport.*

(Above) *Rivers and canals are the true highways and byways of domestic commerce in Burma. The Inland Water Transport Company carries nearly 1.5 million tons and 15 million passengers each year along the country's waterways. Major north-south arteries included the Ayeyarwady, Kaladan, Chindwin, Thanlwin, and Sittoung rivers, all of which feed into vast deltas criss-crossed by navigable streams and canals. Considerable expertise is required to pilot the large riverboats around shifting sandbanks and across changing currents.*

(Right) *In Pyin U Lwin, known among the British as 'Maymyo', the main form of local transport consists of small horse-drawn stagecoaches. At an elevation of 1,070 meters, enclosed carriages suit the town's spring-like climate, while the coaches' turn-of-the-century designs match the faded Tudor mansions built during the colonial era when the British made Maymyo a popular summer retreat. Each is painted according to the individual tastes of its owner.*

While steadily modernizing Yangon and Mandalay receive the bulk of foreign and national investment, village life in Burma's rural areas remains much the same as it has for the last century. Out of necessity, renewable natural products such as leaves and grasses make preferred building materials.

A fisherman on Inle Lake displays the region's unusual talent of 'leg rowing' which frees the hands for handling the cumbersome conical nets used to trap carp. Light industry, such as the production of lye (below) for export to China, Singapore, and Taiwan, has only recently arrived in the countryside.

(Left) *Yunnanese traders—and warriors—from China introduced horses to northern Burma. During larger festivals equestrians are often employed to re-enact famous battles with foreign invaders.*

(Below) *A festival in Mandalay becomes an occasion for farmers to display the prowess of working livestock in bullockcart races.*

52

Elephant working Timber.

An estimated 10,000 Asian elephants (Elephas maximus) make Burma their home—nearly a third of the world count. Over half this number are working elephants used in agriculture and logging, forming the world's largest herd of employed pachyderms. Elephants are so important to everyday life in the jungle that the Burmese language assigns different names to individual males according to tusk shape, e.g., swaigar for wide-spread, upward-curving tusks, hngetpyaw-bu for stumpy, banana-shaped tusks.

(Following pages) An extensive cave complex, ensconced in a limestone cliff overlooking Pindaya Lake, has served as an important Buddhist shrine for centuries. A steep but sheltered, 200-step stairway leads to the cavern entrance, often thronged with worshipers braving thick clouds of incense to pay homage to the 8,094 Buddha images contained inside. Labyrinthian passages connect large caverns with smaller ones, some of which can only be reached by crawling on hands and knees. Visitors strike huge stalagmites dangling from the cave ceiling with wooden mallets to produce booming, gong-like tones.

For Burmese Buddhists, the shin-pyu or Buddhist novitiation ceremony (left) is the most important event in a young man's life. It marks a social passage into puberty, while at the same time providing an intensive training session in Buddhist customs and values. Depending on the resources of the sponsoring families, the procession from home to the village or neighborhood kyaung (monastery) may take place on foot, on horseback, or on elephant. Once the boys reach the monastery they gather in the main hall to listen to a sermon by the abbot and make offerings to the monastic community. They then move to another corner of the compound where the resident monks wash and shave the boys' heads, after which the boys reconvene in the main hall to receive the burgundy-colored robes of novice monks. Thus ordained, each novitiate remains at the monastery for a few days or a few weeks— depending on the wishes of his parents or the recommendations of an astrologer. According to Burmese Buddhist beliefs, parents obtain great kutho (Buddhist merit) when their sons take on robes. While novitiation for Buddhist boys is nearly universal, a similar monastic opportunity is available to girls who choose to become temporary Buddhist nuns. Fewer families send their daughters to a monastery for this purpose; pink-robed nuns, such as these pictured above in Bhamo, must cook their own food for each meal while monks receive daily donations of cooked food from the lay community.

In addition to learning about Buddhist tenets and monastic customs, novitiates may receive basic skills in reading and writing while residing in a monastery (right). For poorer boys in rural areas, monastic stints may form the sum of their formal education.

(Above) *A graceful reclining Buddha image depicts the Enlightened One during his dying moments, as he passes from* nibbana *(*nirvana*) incarnate into the body-less realm of* parinibbana.

(Left) *High above the coastal plains, balanced on the edge of a granite cliff in the Bago Range, the Kyaiktiyo boulder shrine glitters in the unearthly dawn. Legend recounts how a hermit sage hid a hair of the Buddha in his own topknotted hair until he met noble Burmese King Tissa in the 11th century. The sage entrusted the king with the hair, requesting that he enshrine the sacred relic atop a boulder that resembled the hermit's head. The Burmese believe the power of the hair, hidden in the base of the small stupa surmounting the boulder, prevents the rock from teetering off the edge of the cliff. After Shwedagon Paya, Kyaiktiyo is the most sacred Buddhist pilgrimage site in Burma.*

(Right) *Kyaik Pun, on the outskirts of Bago, features four 30-meter Buddhas sitting back to back and is the largest such monument in Burma. Built in 1476 during the reign of beloved King Dhammazedi, all four images display the* bhumisparsa *or 'earth-touching' pose. In this posture the Buddha sits cross-legged with his left hand lying palm up in his lap, the right reaching out to touch the earth with his fingertips. The gesture represents an episode that occurred when Prince Siddhartha—the Buddha-to-be—was on the brink of attaining enlightenment through meditation. When Mara the tempter (a rough Buddhist equivalent to Satan) tried to distract Siddhartha from his meditation, the young prince-turned-ascetic touched the ground to signify that he wouldn't budge from that spot until his objective had been achieved.*

Stupas are solid structures with a square or five sided base. The base is terraced, having three or five levels. Usually from the left keeping the sanctuary on the right and traveling in the same directions as the sun does through the sky. Illustrated here is the plan of Shwezigon Stupa.

SHWEZIGON   PAGODA (plan)

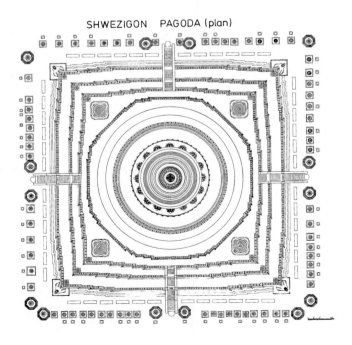

Temples are built with a hollow chamber inside allowing pilgrims to enter for prayers or meditation. The earliest temples usually had a projecting vestibule that led into a hall-like sanctuary. Their design was intended to resemble the interiors of the early Buddhist caves of north India. Later temples employed a central nucleus that was surrounded by a passageway. Extensive design transformations in this latter period led to the development of new construction techniques unknown in the region up to that time: cloister and barrel-vaulting held in position by voussoirs. Illustrated here is the plan of That-byin-nyu Temple.

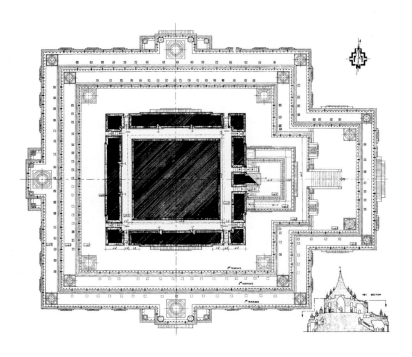

The diversity of Burma's 45 million residents spread over a region stretching over 1300 miles (2000 kilometers) from north to south extends from Tibetans inhabiting the Himalayan climes of northern Kachin State to sea gypsies roaming the tropical waters of the Mergui Archipelago only 9 degrees north of the equator. In between, a 2,832-kilometer coastline supports a huge fishing and marine products industry. Dozens of distinct hill-tribe groups–like this Palaung women (right)–live in the hills bordering Thailand, India and Bangladesh, while ethnic minorities such as these Shan elders (above) sharing food in a village in the northern Shan State, live virtually out of reach of mainstream Burmese society. The Shan people account for around 10% of Burma's population—their name coming from the same Austro-Thai linguistic root as the word 'Siam'; and they are closely related to the Siamese of Thailand and the Laotians of Laos.

(Previous pages) *Along the banks of the Ayeyarwady River, sand miners collect river silt to be used in making cement. In the foreground, vendors make their way toward a riverboat stopping off along the Mandalay-Pyay route. Riverboat passengers often bring their own food for longer journeys.*

(Above and left) *Situated 1,300 meters above sea level in the Shan State, Inle Lake's calm waters extend for nine kilometers through the cleft of a river valley. High hills rim the lake, while the flat lakeshore and lake islands bear 17 villages on stilts. The lake serves as the primary domain of the Inthas, an ethnic group believed to have migrated north from their original homeland near Dawei on the tropical Taninthayi Peninsula. The hard-working Intha are famous for propelling their flat-bottomed teak pirogues by standing at the stern on one leg and using the other leg to push the long oar through the water. This strange leg-rowing technique offers relief to the arms during long paddles from one end of the lake to the other in search of fish. Using huge, cone-shaped nets stretched tautly over wood and bamboo frames, Intha fishermen harvest* nga-pein, *a coveted type of carp, as well as other freshwater fish. Village women weave colorful Shan shoulder bags and silk longyis on wooden handlooms. Every five days the Inthas and Shan convene a floating market in the village of Ywama at the south end of the lake to buy and sell local handicrafts, foodstuffs, and consumer goods.*

(Right) *Ngapali, known as one of the prettiest beaches in the Rakhine State, shares its bounty with local villagers. As the nets are emptied, village women carry the baskets loaded with fish back to their villages, where the catch is divided into three parts: fish to be eaten that day, fish for the local market, and fish to be sun-dried on the beach for later consumption or for far-away markets.*

(Below) *Glazed pots—including the large 'Martaban jars' used to hold water throughout rural Burma—wait for shipment on the banks of the Ayeyarwady River.*

(Above) *A festival-goer in Mandalay keeps her pet parrot happy.*

(Left) *At a rustic toddy bar outside Pyay, friends share an afternoon pot of* htan yei *or 'toddy juice'. Tapped from the leaf stems of living sugar palms in the early morning, htan yei is sweet and non-alcoholic for the first few hours but by early afternoon ferments to becomes a slightly sour, slightly alcoholic beverage.*

Burma's cross-ethnic identity revolves around bamahsan chin or 'Burmese-ness', a common set of cultural characteristics that serves as a social ideal or code of behavior for most Burmese regardless of ethnic background. These include respect for elders, fluency in the Burmese language, familiarity with the Buddhist scriptures, modest dress, discreet behavior toward the opposite sex, and the cultivation of a quiet, subtle, and indirect nature.

Offerings of food, incense, flowers, and candles at the Pindaya Caves assure an accumulation of kutho *(Buddhist merit) for the next life. Most of the gilded wood, marble, stone, lacquer, and brick images found in the Pindaya Caves date to the 18th and 19th centuries, though a few are considerably older. An 18th-century Shan-style sitting Buddha (right) displays the crown, jewelry, and ornate robes associated with royalty—a symbolic reference to Buddha's princely upbringing and his religious status as Rajadhiraja or 'King of Kings'. The simpler sculptures featuring a dome-shaped* ushnisha *(protuberance atop the skull, a mark of enlightenment in Buddhist iconography) hail from 19th-century Mandalay.*

(Above) *Burmese lacquerware, highly prized by collectors, has its origins in an 11th-century technology imported by traders from southern China and northern Thailand. Today Burma's main centers for the lacquerware industry include Bagan, Kyaukka, and Kengtung. After extracting the substance from the* kusum *tree (Melanorrhea usitata), Burmese artisans mix lacquer with paddy-husk ash and apply the substance in layers over bamboo frames to produce light, durable, waterproof containers of all shapes and sizes. Higher quality containers may feature up to seven layers of lacquer and make use of horse-hair as well as bamboo strips for extra flexibility. A well-made bowl can be squeezed till the opposite rims meet, without crack-ing. Artisans paint each lacquer layer separately, and then the piece is incised and polished over a period of days or weeks—even months in some cases—to produce polychromatic works of art.*

(Top right) *A Shan woman spins cotton for the native textile industry. Cotton, a product of northern Burma, is a fabric staple throughout the country; silks and synthetics are for the most part imported from China. Multi-colored cotton longyis and embroidered Shan-style shoulder bags find their way to markets as far away as Bangkok.*

(Bottom right) *A master potter shapes a 'Martaban jar' in Twante, a major ceramics center in the Ayeyarwady River Delta. Artisans typically combine wheel-throwing and coiling techniques to form these utilitarian containers. Afterwards the pots are air-dried in vast thatched-roof potting sheds, then glazed and fired in large walk-in adobe kilns. A busy potter's family can produce as many as 70,000 handmade pots in a year.*

(Left) *In Bagan, a student practices* yok-thei pwe *or Burmese marionette theater. Codified during the late 18th century, classical puppetry exerted considerable influence on other Burmese performing arts, particularly dance-dramas known as* zat pwe *in which dancers depict episodes from the* jatakas *(Buddha life-stories) or India's Ramayana epic.*

(Above) *The most Burmese of all musical instruments is the* saung kauk, *a boat-shaped harp with 13 strings. In addition to serving as a melody instrument within the seven- to 10-instrument* saing—*the traditional ensemble that accompanies classical dance-drama—the Burmese harp occupies an honored role in musical duets with the* michaung *or crocodile lute.*

(Right) *One of the most prominent and best-loved characters in traditional Burmese drama and literature, the red-clothed* zawgyi *represents the mystery and mastery of alchemy. Unlike the European alchemic tradition, in which the alchemist seeks only to transmute base substances into gold or other precious metals, the Burmese* zawgyi *cult believes the correct formula will not only give the alchemist power over the physical world, it will transfer immortality upon his soul.*

(Above) *Shan leaders meet over tea and snacks during a festival. Shan culture recognizes hereditary leadership positions known as* sao pha (sawbwa *in Burmese) and Shan festivals serve as important administrative as well as social events. The Shan State occupies approximately one-quarter of the country's land area. During the British administration of Burma, the state (then divided into several smaller states) enjoyed a large degree of autonomy and today many Shan consider themselves unwilling subjects of Burmese rule.*

(Right and left) *Of the 67 major ethnicities living in Burma, the Karen make up the third most numerous group, comprising about 7% of the total population. Preferring lowland river valleys where they can practice crop rotation, they predominantly reside in Burma's Kayin State—which shares a border with Thailand—and in the delta area of the Ayeyarwady Division. The two major sub-groups, the Skaw Karen and Pwo Karen, can be distinguished by the color and patterns of thickly-woven V-neck tunics that comprise the most significant element of their everyday costumes. The girl in this hand-tinted colonial era photo is Pwo Karen. The Karen are active participants in the jade trade* (left) *often acting as middle men for Chinese merchants who travel from as far as Hong Kong to negotiate purchases*

(Following pages) *The Ananda Temple in Bagan twinkles in the approaching dusk.*

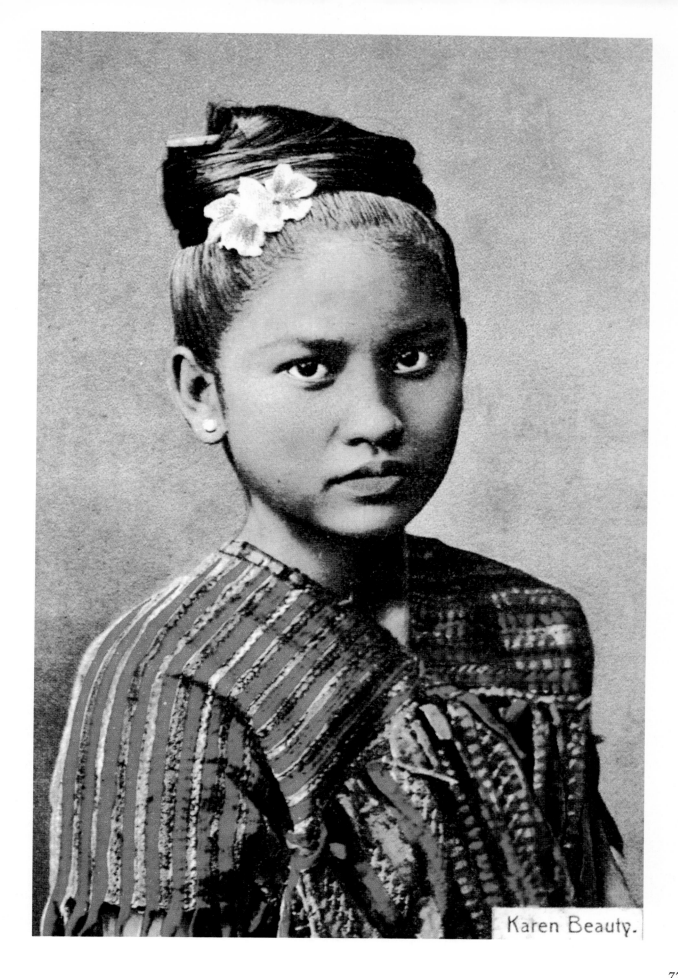

Karen Beauty.